LOS ANGELES

ALSO BY MAUREEN ALSOP

Apparition Wren
Mantic
Later, Knives & Trees
Mirror Inside Coffin

PYRE

PYRE

MAUREEN ALSOP

Copyright © 2021 by Maureen Alsop. All rights reserved.
Published in the United States by What Books Press,
the imprint of the Glass Table Collective, Los Angeles.

Library of Congress Cataloging-in-Publication Data

Names: Alsop, Maureen, author.
Title: Pyre / Maureen Alsop.
Description: Los Angeles : What Books Press, [2021] | Includes index. |
　Summary: "The poems in Pyre are spacious, experimental and abstract,
　delving into collaborations invented in life and life beyond"-- Provided
　by publisher.
Identifiers: LCCN 2021023429 | ISBN 9780984578269 (paperback)
Subjects: LCGFT: Poetry.
Classification: LCC PS3601.L69 P97 2021 | DDC 811/.6--dc23
LC record available at https://lccn.loc.gov/2021023429

Cover art: Gronk, *Untitled*, mixed media on paper, 2021
Book design by Ash Good, www.ashgood.com

What Books Press
363 South Topanga Canyon Boulevard
Topanga, CA 90290

WHATBOOKSPRESS.COM

For Steven

And in memory of Hillary Gravendyk, Joseph Lexa

CONTENTS

Introduction, by Andrew Wessels   11

Selenomancy: A divination by the observation of the phases and appearances of the moon

    Selenomancy: Where the Apparent Wobbling   19
    of the Moon Is Known as Libration

    Selenomancy: Without Surface Pattern   47

    Selenomancy: at Quadrature   53

    Selenomancy: Looking Southward   61

    Selenomancy: When the Apparent Change   69
    in Size Is Due to the Eccentricity of Orbit

    Selenomancy: In Summer Heat   77

Acknowledgments   87
Author's Notes   90
Notes on Collaboration   91
Index of Titles   93

INTRODUCTION

MY FIRST MEMORY OF A PYRE is when I encountered Patroclus's funeral in the *Iliad*. Achilles places Patroclus's body atop the pyre along with the sacrifices of sheep, cattle, horses, oil, honey, the king's dogs, and a dozen sons of his enemies. But the pyre didn't burn. After praying to the gods, the fire finally lit, the body was cremated, and Achilles fell asleep. I've since learned that this isn't the only way to construct a pyre. The body can also be placed underneath or within. This interior approach to pyre-building came to my mind as I read the collection you're holding right now: Maureen Alsop's *Pyre*. In Alsop's hands, the construction of a poem is a process akin to making this second kind of pyre: letters and ink become words, words are arranged into lines, and the lines are combined into language objects that are waiting for us as readers to alight them by reading them. Alsop's poems wait for us to set them alight and burn them into meaning.

This isn't meant to imply that Alsop makes us hunt for some hidden subtext. Rather, the author, the speaker, the addressee, the content—everything we take away from the poem—occurs within the act of reading the poem. "I stand in the sleep of midfield," Alsop writes in "Sacrestia." There is an object—the pyre or the poem—and there is the reason for the object—the body or the meaning we receive from the poem: "Whose / equinox between ghosts" ("{Elegy in Green Abatement: You Designate

Seeing as the Seer}"). The meaning is inside the poem and we experience it by reading.

Pay attention to the pronouns: "When we walked through the boundaries we changed the pronoun" ("Sacrament of Venus"). Pronouns provide a fulcrum where the matter of language becomes energy: "When I speak to the ghost inside our ghost, you are spared" ("Blackout"). The pronouns here hold multitudinous meanings. The "I" is Alsop as author, you, and myself as reader. "Our" is an Alsop-me, an Alsop-you the reader, and also an Alsop-addressee. "You" is all of the above, and whoever we as readers direct that pronoun toward as we make the poem our own. The physical matter of these pronouns, the ink on the page, burns up into energy and light. And what makes this powerful to a reader is that we can see and experience multitudes of emotional amplitude. Alsop is mourning the loss of her loved ones, and through the vessels of the pronouns we see that and we are given a pyre to remember and honor our own losses: "We were those who live against fire's spine" ("Sky an Oar, XXV/IV/MMXIV").

I'm leaning into this metaphor of the pyre and the poem, but I have a confession to make: I'm a metaphor sceptic. I do love a well-crafted figurative image. But that love reveals itself most when the metaphor breaks down and reveals something even more true about the tenor and vehicle. Where pyre and poem break down is in the concept of repeatability. A pyre is made for a single occasion and, once burned, ceases to be. While a poem might also be written initially for a single occasion, after being written and published, the poem as an object sustains. Alsop's poems can be read again and again, by the same and new readers. They can be returned to and continue to generate new meanings: "Not portraits, not holy fire, but three messages the trees mouthed in accordance" (p 67).

As I write this brief introductory note, we are about two weeks from the one-year anniversary of the start of the pandemic. Over two and a half million people have died from the virus worldwide. This is a year of loss, of mourning, of emptying, of leaving. In a sense, a pyre is something that is already gone. The dead have already died. The kindling has already died. It is all already gone, and then it goes even further when it's burned. The matter that has built it — logs, kindling, fuel — becomes visible as it turns from matter into light and heat, and the ritual is complete, and it all ceases to be. Alsop's poems are gone, then they go, then they go even further, and they take us exactly where we need to go yesterday, today, and tomorrow, and they are always with us, again and again, as the ritual we need: "Grief is a careful telling of one's written name" ("Sehnsucht").

    Andrew Wessels
    Tuesday, March 2, 2021

The antique hills half far, my fingers salted, stone rosettes cling to my

anklet. Palm trees wave seaward. Suppose

the silt of the river travelled the valley: the full lake renounced the heat:

birch in the heartland of surrounds: and we were not enough to be held.

Shut one admission, against forest, sorrel. Empty handed

in the doorway. Geraniums dried between every other battle;

light remained unnatural. Without stillness you surrendered

as if entering a new descent. Snow seizure. Quiet pages.

You turned the lane loose with white.

O improbable green, my origin—consider
language as light's infrequency. Gray emulsion
of winter over silver rivers and tombs—What

indefinite articulate, the sun's assiduous shape, tends
the horizon's glaze. When I returned home,
the skeletal silence, my gratitude, was a blue ash
touched to the forehead. You

carried buckets of oat. And wordless, let water
anoint the flank of a horse that led you
through cypress groves' narrow secrets. You followed
the bells of a mixed space, toward gate & straw
into a vastness beyond sound. Among the travelled
You are the long travelled. The suddenness

love chose in particulate, a constant I held
as earth claimed my smallness.

SELENOMANCY
WHERE THE APPARENT WOBBLING OF THE MOON IS KNOWN AS LIBRATION

In the year of ghost-holly-noon in winter and chestnut sky at night—
the dead's voices carry dowry-bells and silver spools
along the river's collarbone.

So emerald the quiet. Only shadow in green undertow.

A stone glows a black fire in the small woods, her mouth— drags
slow—the language into a terrain divided by sun: a valley
of tree-casts, check points.

When she stumbled he wiped the taste of moth from her lip. The creek
curdled in heat.

Already masses of lily shift the breeze. She fades halfway
above   and begins.

Dear Hillary,

The sentient wrote seven times loose italic drafts matted in silverfish.
Or saline.

You would not wait as the horses' chest stiffened the pine's shade, for the blue eclipse, for conscription, a carriage as Jet Ski across the burnt bay. Feather chandelier overhead a cloud-dress—an ever-singular carousel this tideway.

They spoke for guidance to each ship that paused: Search, Tanker, Navy. Slow but not slowly I wander our last country. Foreigner I am what's given. Until a single Sunfish sail pierced the corner of my left eye. No mistake the coral-map. No mistake alveoli in slipknot. Told me you were who. No mistake. A scar smudged every quill.

Your shorthand is braided—as when we sat, backs to the windowsill where the sun-dappled spruce bleached the rug and spun the room's island into archipelago. We speak again once in open arrival.

Love, Maureen

P.S. No kidding. My favorite hobbies are archery and stamp collecting. And lumens titrate a prairie's unmet constellation, beyond which stagnant boots cloud the gnats, motes infiltrate the nightcurtain, consume the valley's F-rocks as a withholding of mire; where F is fenestrate, a tumbleweed event-horizon.

SEHNSUCHT

Do what you can, but in case you have need, begin with water. The labradorite underleaf, the shaded eucalypt approbations. No one will defend you. But you will receive touch point. Wander through grasses and consider. What voice holds the rope tightly? Do what you would to guide a somnambulist. Grief is a careful telling of one's written name. Love's clumsy dialogue. Hold no translation. Hold no convention.

BLACKOUT

When I speak to the ghost inside our ghost, you are spared. We drink plum
champagne; listen as ginger bees' melodious scores swarm our laughter. Your
giardiniera of late summer conserve: kumquat, clove, sycamore scent.
Witness, you read the sky's seam as botanical impress. Despite being led
to this, nothing led us here. We followed glass shoreline's effortless shoal.
A frayed sail at cliff's edge. Your eye turned away. The body, without
intimation, recorded an imagined stillness.

Inside the snow my ghost trekked north. Architectures just shy of meadows—
as you crossed a landscape's furrowed constellation. Everything shameless.
We ascended dusk. Meaning, my archetype's unkempt gleam flattened
to moss beneath battened currents. I set a lantern upon the wet grass.

BALLAST

In the veiled light, the chest is a shroud
    for what used to linger, powdered wing
    and circle of flames   destination
mapped my understanding—
        gaps at the waterfront where the ships slowed
to listen to the gulls' song bodies

O, this close to the sea
    The salt covers everything
    like a stuttering glass garden
    at the turn of winter

The women crouch in the sand
    wrestling shells from the insistent shoreline

My pocket flooded with charms
Dusk drawn dawn, moth hour—
venerated faces balance outside the window—

The day's failed confession
    A black stone on the tongue.

SACRAMENT OF VENUS

When we walked through the boundaries we changed the pronoun. She passed: one black carriage; the mare's caution denied by automaticity. Her love reminded you of seven seasons, sixty-seven Galilean moons. She was of germination. Atheist green. It was a private activation, a slow shepherding into the outer world. Her lips a stray of chicory, stinging nettle. Orchid streams. At night you read the weed's summation. Cottonwood's stardust messages abandoned the mustard-rock corridors. Trillium's overgrowth conceded. There is no word for the theories of disjunction, the knowing of snow without atmosphere.

PROMISED

The disillusionment is plain. Errors furred by illness in animal spell. A sham on wishes. Certain messages shut every door. Anger is a truth grievers abide. And the left ones, with their day's imprint, can't separate themselves from her exit. She was promised an impression twice made.

Oh, her voice knew the street home. Knew wishes locked in a wordless room.

Before she went fearless, her travelled voice was without distance. Yes, promises unbridled terrain, as the country we once loved sweats.

There are blows named without emphasis. There are walls engraved.

Earth's brittle predilection. Snow fever, mirror's fervency. Similar, the grass.

Further from dream, but with greater accuracy, the body's punishment expires without impunity. A contrail's chaff smooths the sun. Sky erases the steady spasm. Perhaps she tells.

And comes there, with her eye to the darkness, to separate the cold.

SNOW PARADIGM

I remember crocus tips like pink mimeographs create their method,
and an uncertain resemblance: two girls under the pines
at dusk.
        They imagine a door, struggle with its lock, then wander
onto a path of soft gray needles arms twined, eyes fogged.

You said the gray was absolute   But
    at the beginning of the nineteenth
century a boatman waved his rifle over the Natchez Trace—
        being quite alive the girls held ground
to a translucent square   cottonwood leaves lit a thousand tongues

        panting in the muggy air tasting fire. The river

curled like a finger   around its sloping banks

mustard weed and lambs ear   underfoot

You wore homespun and satin slippers   I was there

when the light fell

The other way to write an elegy is to recount the day's translucence spread. You borrow the earth, tagged by sky's unaccounted edifice. Moon streaked oblation. Erasures were cinquefoil stains, birds as ampoules. Clouds still the freeway in conversation rather than convention. Astringent grasses bade vellum plains. Because we were listening. Because each early clairvoyance spoke the body's unused language: magpie, salt. What was the question?

ARCHIVAL SPARROWS

A new bald cloud. Length of my palm. Slow in the wind's square mirror.

The sky wheel continues. Smolder, grace. Terror. Milton says she will find her way. But I say the lightkeeper divides us. Sea lavender, basal harmonic: this geography, the body's immersed compression. After death was it so much better? Skeletal country; voices tapped cerulean and pinyon. Water: swamp: Clay-color: Dusky: English.

Do you remember she said no boundary bothered her? It was never too late. You dashed the gluestick. Larksky study. Struck plans across every aerial. Silicon witch. Teeter deer. Elemental blues exposed; those witches were carried a long time. Prototype. Like you who. Unafraid, forgave ancestral bruises gentler. Brine engulfed each bird's anatomy.

SEPIOLITE
for Jody Lexa

The air calcified more than once. You're still at the gate. As your
counterpart affirms your senses—a glance backward, a strange
ghost at the table.

Incantations recur through blackthorn: reticulated hazel
one route, the ravine's oceanographic sleep
another. A most sure

mercy you would tell us. You saw yourself time this. This time intimacy

leveled without waking. Weightless loom. Your eyes tracked forests,
ancestors' disjunction, cottonwood corridors.

We lay love's concordance, your voice. Every why now not placed is.

GUARDIAN, BLUE, INEZ

A moment ago he was breathing over a book

And yet only the lamp dull light was witness—a fold where papers stuck. A current between mantlepiece portraits he did not hear.

She only remembered you were at the old house; halfway up the oak stairwell she remained thankful. She remembered love, but that love had faded. She waited at water level— illuminate. His lesser glance turns the pages. Where you found the green grass soft faded.

WITNESS

In the bay they began with candles; mangroves spilled with cranes
and the air of nature readied to turn against you. Red bellflowers sing
through plankton. Love's extol.

Upon the mariner's sleepless noon, you left us straight.

A village across the waters burned all night. Gentle figures carried
halos' sheen, and small boats fanned out against star's trajectory
northward. A shirt sinks in the reef. A blackening mountain
eclipses blue staghorn. My isthmus to your scent of frost and wool.

Hour crosses hour.

On this inlet, larch seem associative—a scripted graveyard.

Your specter culminates the lake's druzy agate; holds dendrites
in one guardian's lung. Ocean's name once: river. Temporal rain once distinct
as sign—phalanges imprints, a pewter moss. I sink heat's sphere against
canopies of terns. I linger.

GHOST ARTICULATE

Tell me which village was a likeness? Necessities were not much
beyond cinquefoil.

The boat, a shy resin, slipped lichen's dock house moss as a striped tongue.
He read oak-umber pages. The blazed star was something he gave
me. I gave him asphalt currents.

The oar gilded water's narrations. Candor, alga. A connecting reflection
between our breath. Unlike me, he could only remember—
O fallow architect, O lily.

PARENTHESIS SKYLINE

All manners pass briefly through you—
                    Eastern Light   Mirabella   Sweet Lilac

A ghost elicited from a blessing that ash conceded. You roam
one end of the corridor to the next

Tutti Frutti   Pink Tonic   Ballerina   Rose Moiré   Frission

Variations in snow: Emprise: shadow: Particuliére: shade: Bel-Argus

The landscape's countless adjustments   asked you unnoticed—

Marquee:
        *Holiday * Distraction * April * Coromandel * Cinema *

Thankfully   one brief curtain frames you—

      in blue pearl   vertigo   black satin—

But this was not the matinee we imagined, auteur,
      —the toxin birds swooped anxieties between horizons
            and the unseen winnowed accidents through us—

But the error was really the sky. Beige. Quartz. Frenzy.
Glue formed the needled stars. They clustered us. Our syntax
was damaged. A pierced liquid. I do not account so clearly the sheen
off their feather's wet hull.

The keeper read our tiny, thinning book: a series of groves where
caution trees accorded our speech. Pages
                              reached the unwelcome edges.
Later, at the house, a ghost caught slightly in the haze. A child-falcon
or the insignificant movement of cloud. We were walked across an uncertain sea.

                                Starlet   May   Paparazzi

JANUARY ITINERARY, PARENTHESIS

Perhaps it was a clearing, ironwood doubled beyond switchback. One drawer
after another opened: adolescent compositions, train ticket stubs; west's
silvering notation scrimmed a buck's skull blanched and sculpted
by the grove's indistinct spires. What question was I, not who, not kindness.
But a physical concentration, late season's lake-effect, snow—

NORTH CHANNEL

This late surface message— H, I hear fireflies alight coal—
      Sumac claims the throat. Now dreams are supplications
and stray horses—

blades our blackened tongues sing beneath keels.

You were the one left in the valley between our language. Waves where

dry grass disposes an expectant green. We spoke of sable stars.

Rusted oranges illuminate the landscapes we hide between. In obsolescence
aluminum trees whisper necessity. O unearthly signal. It is this remembrance
I remember: cosmologies imaginary bodies. I write among light's
moth-pale scatter.

And incorrect as always, I reply to your ghost.

SCURVY, BIRDS

The soul had other ideas while we proclaimed blond
brilliantly in this umber season of molten rust. Arriving
at the door, itself a bronze medallion. Snow's centerfold
was a sedge meadow

               creased with wildflowers. We gathered our hands
together in a brocade bouquet, milk-cloud sky brimming with charms—

We were offered safe passage, handle
shaped like a horn, our hands before
sun-defeated contrails were chrysanthemum blossoms

separating our eyes from the outer body.

What artifice, what control! The air thrumming
with startled sounds, the body quiet as a page.
A silver tabletop laid with cards, but our unwieldy
communion finished with illegible spades. Sparrow's
eggshell, comfrey stem, toast crust. A wintry caul
netted the pink afternoon.

EQUULEUS

This hideaway nebula: calculable as method. Western ratio; ration, myth. Bush rue, mistletoe. A limpid border demarcates palm trees. You travelled inside the screen lugging jugs of cherry vinegar. O sublingual address, please speak. My station. In the wheeling I was a slash mark the sun held open. Sonorous portico. Vellum envelops vellum. A furrow where the boundary deepens into sky when you close your eyes. Lucid, parcel-shape cloud: cirro cumulo stratus. Something ~~~~~~~ (like this), but not so.

SKY AN OAR, VII / XII / MMXIV

The dark said that things could go on loving. Moss grew up the drain
and Roman grasses reflected June's long window; shadow's sun inside
shadow's shadow. She shared,
        before the ocean rendered cobalt, what she could.   The ghostly

walking away with her gloves, up the stairs
somewhere into the old night. The night that is kind.

What so now I wonder. What sleep's dreamless trek of snow. What easy first
breath made last and whose as whole. Without our lowest guard
of pride. We eased the time before the tracery bells beneath the sea seemed
perfectly new, and noon's intermediary horizon rose into discourse.

WHERE GLASS SHORE'S LIGHT WAVERS

The sun-sketched ravine cultivates no distinction for light.
In an interview, the subtlety of the underbody justified a soft slow aquatic—
                         and a mud swamp screened by cattail thickets.

The apparition did not announce herself.
She lay on the foot of the rumpled bed, dress tattered.
         Without diffidence I asked what it was I could do—

Repose cooled the yellow-wooded mesquite,
                         not quite off-white, as she left with her linens.

River birch muscled galactic thresholds,
         and avocet's mirage cowered above the dense salt-flat.

ANOTHER WAY TO SAY YOUR NAME

I was the cause and the effect of ghosts—what I carried in my hand: hawthorn horizon's contrails.

[A Few Facts About the Name Maureen]

So you go wither. Mid-dusk flattened to moss.

Diminutive, Mo

I take the crumpled pages that I love from the book of love and I must love them again and again. I read the last card near the hill as men came to stare at the shadow between us.

[The Meaning of the Name is 'The Sea' or 'Bitter']

The doorway is a stream upon night aspens, weeds wink. I am kept by this rifle. I am spared.

Latin Meaning, Dark

Ash in the midline folds her lovingly.

*

> *This is what I took,*
> *the bark cloth, the animal*
> *weight, velveteen blue hues,*
> *panoramas reeled as appetites*
> *and imaginings fell away.*
> *Half awake I redesigned*
> *the pattern—visceral, unkempt.*
> *Grass in the whispered*
> *surrounds leaks a dry glow; a*
> *kestrel's inscription…….*

*

Not even the one who is reckless, named as darkness, knows fervor; knows, before death, the moment earth shimmers.

{WHY LOSS BURNS BACK THE ONLY ACCOMPANIMENT OUR NAME HARDLY SAVES}

We waited in the zone of forgetting
Warming tincture in a tin pocket
And pedaled furiously when the door opened

Soaked sugar cubes extracted a kind of fire
As if taking back summer's long rhythm

Or demanding a tympanic line
Something to rouse and rabble
Something to secure a wisp of blue smoke

As when flames over whiskey curve into lavender undulations
The snake of our too-close approximations

Reminiscent of lilac-silver-maple- supplications
We are carved from instinct
Knowing that liquid itself sanctifies a storm's condition

So your heart up close is the truth

GLOSSOPETRAE

I sit up straight ask for space within her congenial grove. Before pain's absence moth's infected the gloam. Her vessel came, low twilight. No sea. No city. No man's sky. Starred with damage the body what was left to tell.
A mirror shone refused language, the last moon slipped. As to the dreaming, craft lightened one moment— then another left.

But if it troubles you, now in gladness, the moss-lit edge, this scratch across the eyelid, lark's skeletal procession, she wanders fates resolute placebo where yesterday we carved statues for the gods.

The half-folded page was my only means of knowing you were alive.

SELENOMANCY
WITHOUT SURFACE PATTERN

Dear Forgiveness,

Yesterday from the valley of lagoons I heard them. They were shot
in the adjoining room where silt sprayed the glass wall—not so far beneath
the earth. Summer's sizzled grasses bent upward through floorboards
& a strange witchery hung like pollen's afterbite.

A green portico broke open above the bottle trees and now I could see
water's ruins beneath the blackwood, weed & thistle.

Our hereafter lives— the very last day—
My briefcase papers askew, our contracts splayed across the field.

Someone lost us at the exit—you held a jackknife softly against my forearm—
something left my skin— I knew the blade was a lake I once swam in— black
elms bowing under currents, fray of pine needles netting the shore.

I did not know, I could not dream. What part of you remained.

There was one sentence left on the page.

I was the trauma inside betrayal, the elm tree's secondment

to sea from field. Code-switching, I parted the grass. When the lungs

settle there is a betoken ringing, a holy sphere where the meadow-body

lay. I was in love with the season's alarm—

        transparent blossoms, snow's reckoning.

CRIMES TONIGHT

Into the tell of it I asked. The grass tugged at the river. Once
the blindman. Once the mirror's foam. I followed your image: weed,
trail, song. This was survival. Itinerant face, I was warned into the falling
mountain. But consider this. Consider we could only dream doors open
to finish. Meanwhile each city we passed burned under that same old sun.

This was our knowledge: tainted, coal-colored wing, a sky infused powder?

A city you troubled by blink. Aspect, what

was yours? Did you, as everything you stated—night's

scarlet speedwell, bottlebrush, imaginary waters, mnemonic green,

a bruised wheel—render and await the bereaved

whose circumstance is seen.

SELENOMANCY
AT QUADRATURE

What spell learning offers as when your boat recedes. You tell yourself *strike dear* and traverse auburn currents, cedar scented reeds. You lean. Past horses dead against mountain's gleam. As you once appeared below language.

This year's snapshot-dull sky drags ahead anchored by mute arrows; starling's contrails flicker a hapless boundary. But this is after. After the outer body where we mapped this impartial door. After the twenty-ninth fold. After asphalt' celestial scuff. Father, I apologize. The slept warmth,
the snow. The dark toward rooms untouched.

PROTHALAMION

I fingered our forecast, the wind conjured a horse. You
        cupped my face in your hands, replayed the dusk-small girl
who eyed the hundred dead. Rust-colored clouds

mottled our edges—and we, in the waxing phases, heat of our heart, walked
hand in hand into snow-covered avenues. But our eyes did not speak. Perhaps
that song: the reeds in a loom following street-fire. Our spells

repeated. We rode through milestones where devil's sparrow flocked
the grass. Did you believe in predilection?

{MIDNIGHT BOTANICA: THE TEMPLE IS REACHABLE ONLY BY A BRIDGE}

The night, as in sun dead, father. All black the blackening has been. As in mourning. The faces of light along the road, once with your reflection, turn hardwood for stone. Quiet my privations as early breath, as water. Still the living move through us. A slow glacier in the lung, as blue is.

MATINS FOR JULIET

Temporal, the deer, your animal self curled down, moss-sheltered
& tenuous. It was an easy knowledge: yellow blossoms motionless smoke
gathered in the reeds. Snow's reversal, brevity, a shapely whiteness
of shutter & wench. This is as it is. An intimate mercy.

SKY AN OAR, VIII / XI / MMXVI

Krishnamurti said when the one you love goes, a part of you follows. Typewritten gnats spill greasy birdseed tunnels. For a moment there are two worlds. Spring presses toward me through glass; my garden hallway, a clutter of spiders in milky silt. Crocus unpin your breastbone. In all eventual acts, humans compose ghost.

SKY AN OAR, X / XII / MMXIV

I occupy a small settlement on the lake–a lung shaped house
of stucco & asphalt. Here, bird halos lean outward—early acidic stars,
the sky's skull-yellow surface. Very alone. I listen as your touch
& untouch go blank.

Snow's synthesis falls.   What light there is
I make the most of: a damp planet blinks beneath banksia. Radio waves
pitch your arrival. Slowly slowly your words came. One found one. Your
last earthward year. You orbit love's old battalion, bushfire, space where
meadow clings to wind.

SELENOMANCY
LOOKING SOUTHWARD

At the old house we mulch gray pachysandra & peony—atremble of sticks,
stasis, sandalwood cinder. At his burial's many places we ask where
we would find him, how we would remember his name.

Green frost under the sun as we enter the aborted orchard. Spared bees stifle
a circadian heat—afterlife's adaptation, or a passive threat. He hid
above the pasture. Stood, in fact, open, in the presence of his lover; while

in the next century the room filled with brine and we cleared
the table. I hold then what I never loved—shadow grass lodged
in the lung, nightingale's spate noon. But we didn't read
April's breath within our own. I stood

within sound's aura and watched an aster's pale architecture exit fern's
undergrowth. Spindrift voices. Kestrel's counsel
followed us like firebombs through the grove.

SKY AN OAR, XXV / IV / MMXIV

We laundered our t-shirts in the citadel. An animal bond to a keeper.
How do you record dark's finery of unstitched hem. Drop by drop the night
fell in love with it's own indifference. O, Tender Conductor, do you
remember your name. Botany's secret

is a mural of constellations, remedies soiled roots, and mistakenly
I'd abandoned a leaf's indigo socket, but there and there each acre
became a horse's master. We were those who live against fire's spine.
I wish I'd never seen that country tangled in smoke,
or any war possessed by doubt.

GABION

Beautiful it is when you say I am. As when
an army unloads a basket of stones. Unsteady
        shoreline or fence line. Our
invisible boundary mapped by water-edge & light.

AGGREGATE TURNING EVERY ASPEN

We found summer: a clear lavender border, where
                              solemn shoals and clouds secede as view.
Two ghosts in larch outline musicality—
                              the wind crafts or shakes—
Suspended or invented, the landscape's sequence
                              does not recognize our subtle shades.

You rode by horseback, the white thicket,
                              a beige predicament bound as brocade, not snow.

The kingbirds quarreled the raven, a mosquito haze,
                              the season's secret opiates.

SACRESTIA

I stand in the sleep of midfield. Beyond ancient grass, grief's mercy: voices in paragraphs of sugary sedition, self-conscious brevity. I died in a burning sweat, a wheeze of smoke between bramble. Strong enough to escape fever, you left a glass cup at the windowsill. Smoothness like thirst. Light's last conspirator. Before you let go your hand.

LATER STAR, LATE BLACKNESS

Linden shadows expand the room. An old creosote. Or bland window. Now against the stairs. To a place one passage flosses a drawn figure. Stillness. The night is thinking. As a lark scars the sky bound sleek into sun's hush. O darling. O, Eridanius. No, the furthest river *does* recognize us.

SELENOMANCY
WHERE THE APPARENT CHANGE IN SIZE IS DUE TO THE ECCENTRICITY OF ORBIT

Dear Hope,

The first of the season inverts the sun. You left her when snow's miscarriage
entered the room—her body explored love's copyright and wandered the river.
Because we disagreed on the landscape's grammar. Someone edited the sea
that night. Someone crosshatched the forest. She was convicted. Not numb. But
so you went. Outside, a greening milk

lessened the leaves and woolen vines. You failed to witness gold's last runnel
redress violet. Twilight fingered the grass. Let's remember she warned you.
The nightjar's churr, a far distraction, repeated. I was watching you fail. We both
knew someone who died at the weir last Christmas, but let's forget that trouble.
She inserted the glass along the rusty edge of the frame. She was not helpless.
I saw her outline. In the rain her hair looked red.

Through the walls I resumed my hatred. Your blade's very curve crossed
my neck—you were not my lover, but an other now—it was like solstice
by touch—the cold reflected off granite and I saw the trail backward where
the new ones travelled. A metal scream poured from my throat. What words came,
came in pieces. I'm sorry for the lamp spreading a net of insects
across the elm, and the means by which the men approached. You lay
your light on me in secret.

Breathing into the next nearness   snow in the night
the holy otherness of rain—

shows us
each bound to air— a waiting darkness

{ELEGY IN GREEN ABATEMENT: YOU DESIGNATE SEEING AS THE SEER}

We will press love's thistle into thumb. We will love without
shade. O temperance. O blur sky's
    swarm   stings   muscle wide.   Night

falls back into destructive eyes. Salt the lamp. Lapse was not
              the sound the omen loosened into the swift.

Nor fallacy's variations: horse among deer grass—

    a secret faded. Whose equinox between ghosts? Whose wheel?

What rope did you bring.

CHALMETTE {THROUGH JUNE IN DRY PLACES, GENERIC NAMES}

The day is a long grass we wade. Heat scars our shins. Bells & architectures blaze uncertain constellations. I remembered our death. Milk greased snow. We observed the form of their method as a means. Shadow's floor shaped discourse. Words traced patterns as wounded crocus. Syllables lashed blossom to the boundary. So we might forgive. This country we considered personal.

*

We never traversed a battlefield   only calculated a space where thugs, edge line, oil stains mapped epidermal layers.

*

Small sensualities held the bereaved in view. O unmet tomb, imagined fingerling. Paper held body. A sketch of sleeves, a fiddle neck. Corsage: view one, view two—

view i

Unrecognizable, she lay. Crumpled silk dress, wet hemline off the river. An amalgam of sawdust held her body as a sketch. I asked you? Fingered her sleeve's texture. Asked also, advancing, what force her thread. And why from this dream, that marsh she woke.

view ii

As it was within the centaury florets, covered in pollen, I am paragraph's flax.

A bell's palelight does not reach. It was soft, but without

the sound of your voice. Tugged threads—my meadow-skirt rustled.

SKY AN OAR, XIII / XII / MMXIV

She never talked about the accident, but this was a lie she presented
as apology. What she saw crawling crawled itself back: A moth's alacrity
against dull headlight, a cold assemblage—not chrome but a residue
where lung-light filled the glass. At the hospital

they thought her tender. As when a soldier's victory seeds new seductions
and one can rename the unnamed horse half-buried in the eastward field.

That morning her shadow walked past and sat at your breakfast table,
and the scent of your pipe primed the typing-desk's every drawer. Only
parchment could answer. Unconvinced she followed you through heath
to find herself heal. Until your sputtering went underground and her lung's
moss archways bricked the forest floor—you held her alone hand, a faded
lupine, your pearlweed lips grazed bloodwood fingertips, her torso spelled
a new boundary. Scat in the snow grove. As it happens. As the hour's total
heat is a frailty—at which point winter-tracks, pines, the reply of bells
are a stochastic system, the latest foreground, aqueducts numbed outline.

You cursed her and you cursed her. Yourself cursed self.

SELENOMANCY
IN SUMMER HEAT

I've stolen the sea. Come hell of the tide. O Guardian's shadow, O milkwood
highway through the kingdom, I swam the valley salt flats as you left
the frame—the night space, air's brushstroke in cyclone—

Snow touched the travellers' shoulders when David stood between
the troops. The authorities drew sides. I lowered. I lay as I lay in the world—
sword touching the throat, an angel inside the tip. See what you like he said.
So I saw, and he met me under the storm tree. This was always
the law of my discipline: a shooting of orders, banksia's bronze
branches, a chandelier of cheated leaves.

The grass hums as revenants whiten my father's grave and ether rings
in the cedar; this is not the noise of a coward—above me—but my mother, my
air by my side. Home drawn into me. A few times breath omits breath. Now
moths circulate my lips— heavy stars sleep in celebration.

I forget their words, that field, my battle.

This is another way to stay the line—

SOFTLY

Underneath the grass atmosphere, a carriage crosses us. Observes you. As if we are a flicker of leaves, fire's scent.

Above, I've seen her face in the clearing. Her aster palette eyelids lowered—two small shimmering crescents gazed into a clean reflection. Then outward over the bright lawn. I think she saw nobody, but heard as if in a wide room […connection glitch…] —She insists, her mineral description. But loosened.

I believe it was simply birds singing.

PONTIAC

You only believed loved ones claimed certain fields and in fields where
your loved ones were claimed, only of snow, your belief.

When you passed between burials, she named you ghost. Unlike you
she didn't wait. The merciless sun's bead

upon your back wouldn't yield. You wished

to forget this or wished to forget what
was there before she began. Suppose

she was you. Without any theory or season. Suppose it was midnight
in the small center of town, your name uttered by the lips of soldiers.

It's late now. Counsel your thirst.
A circle of flies guides your brow.
Addition by subtraction.

Along the cliffs ice dark sparks as pine blossoms early.

OCULUS

Were the screens between constellations innumerable at that point you saw
yourself? I've heard the entrance there is infinite. Whose providence
leads you? Grief, or an opposite dusk.
—O, ill-educated lover.   — O, penitent sovereign. — Traveler
please investigate the midland. Where the prairie's nitrogen-blue exhaust
filled your lungs; where the breezeway departs it's sky. Spirit after spirit
waits.   O, necessary one. Finalize your checklists: evaporative particles,
theoretical dimensions. You carry an old work, grayed into animal spectre,
amenable sheen as in a summary. Mercury's halo is somehow struck
dumb. You abide the anchoress as now observed in stereoscope. No, you were
not invulnerable. You were a slowly shame's slowly-ness turned ghostward.

Not portraits, not holy fire, but three messages the trees mouthed in accordance. When guard units beat swords into your prone neck I came to work for you on another plane. Your afterlife's translation was my language's reversal. You were my lover inside my betrayal. On the next page: green's pre-fevered breath pollutes the flame.

TÁIM SÍNTE AR DO THUAMA

On the day of the battle you said to me, in simple command under goshawk's convocation: *when you get there do not cross.*

But I followed the landscape down through an animal's lingual gesture. Bodily. Without allegiance. Through the last grove's blackened pine, I forged cinder's undercurrent across the gorge. I lay my hands on the soldier's ribs and in unison smooth out the jaundice oak leaves where his body lay—as if each impression might circulate bell, book and candle.

The pious grit their teeth—wade through the 17th-century walls behind me—every time I hear any song. And I always say, 'Sinead would sing that so much better'… It's a fact.

APPRENTICE

Salt chalked in aspen. Snow's depth. Minus motes against stone walls where wisps confuse our form. Cold clasps. The light, glass wrists littered in bangles, a wheeze. Sulfur scented wind. Intelligible even in exile. I hear you listen.

SKY AN OAR, XXXI / VII / MMXVI

If you are to guide the dead you are to work the night's quick orbit. Yes, there is another way to die—bee's breath, cosmology of shade's witness—a sense of heat as you lean into the horizon's blue scuff: here distant swallows wheel an uncertain margin. Of the five instructions: never farewell a saint at dawn.

                        and when the hour leaves   and my body
is taken from you—

Passover bells will measure the sparrow's polished note, you'll hear ammunition through an open door

  I will ask   in all my gathering

              how would you have me leave—

It will take a city of unfurnished rooms until you enter the one where blue headlights break the windows into trees

Follow the sun's physicality which lies upstairs in dream figures

I am the aftertell

                    I am sleeping

                                      Over the last world

ACKNOWLEDGMENTS

Gratitude to the editors and publishers who supported the publication of these poems:

Anomaly: "Dear Hillary (The sentient wrote …)."

burntdistrict: "Crimes Tonight."

concis: (VIII/XI/MMXVI) "Krishnamurti said when the one you love goes…"

Coldfront (Poets Off Poetry): "Táim sínte ar do thuama," a response to "You Are Stretched on My Grave."

Connotation Press: "Selenomancy in Summer Heat," "Selenomancy Without Surface Pattern," "and when the hour and my body are taken from you—…."

Diagram: "Matins for Juliet."

Escape Into Life: "January Itinerary, Parenthesis" (written in collaboration with Lissa Kiernan; Lissa's poem titled "Perhaps It Was a Clearing").

Existere: "Oculus" and "Witness."

Foundry Journal: "Sky an Oar," VII/XII/MMXVI" and "Sky an Oar, XXV/IV/MMXVI."

Glint Literary Journal: "Sacrestia."

Helen: A Literary Magazine: "She never talked about the accident…" and "I occupy a small settlement on the lake—a lung shaped house…."

Lost Roads [Lines]: "The disillusionment is plain…."

A New Ulster: "Guardian, Blue, Inez," "The Other Way," "Sehnsucht," "Sincerely."

Oracle Fine Arts Review: "{Midnight Botanica: The Temple Is Reachable Only by a Bridge"}."

Poetry Salzburg Review: "Chalmette {Through June in Dry Places, Generic Names}."

Rascal: "Selenomancy Looking Southward."

Tuesday; An Art Project (Lucky 13 Issue): "Sacrament of Venus."

Volta: "Ballast," "Scurvy, Birds," "[Why Loss Burns Back the Only Accompaniment Our Name Hardly Saves]," "Snow Paradigm," and "Blackout" (previously "Dear Hillary, When I speak to the ghost inside our ghost, you are spared….").

Zone 3: "Sky an Oar, XXXI/VII/MMXVI."

"Ballast," (written in collaboration with Hillary Gravendyk), "Selenomancy Looking Southward" (written in collaboration with Brenda Hammack), and "January Itinerary, Parenthesis" (written in collaboration with Lissa Kiernan also appeared in *A Multi-Genre Anthology of Contemporary Collaborative Writing* (Black Lawrence Press), edited by Simone Muench and Dean Rader.

"Selenomancy: Where the Apparent Wobbling of the Mood is Known as Libraton" appeared in the anthology: *The Night's Magician: Poems about the Moon* (Negative Capability Press), edited by Sue Brannan Walker and Philip Kolin.

Untitled poems "Suppose the silt of river . . . " "Shut one admission . . ." (initially titled "Preliminary") appeared in the anthology: *Thirty Three* (Negative Capability Press), edited by Sue Brannan Walker.

"O improbable green. . ." (initially titled "Croquis for the Etruscan") appeared in the anthology *Menacing Hedge: A Limited Edition Anthology for AWP 2015*, edited by Kelly Boyker and Craig Wallwork.

In gratitude to: Hillary Gravendyk, Brenda Hammack, Lissa Kiernan, and Matteo Lexa for creative and collaborative joy;

to Cynthia Arrieu-King, Megan Estrella, John and Katherine Gravendyk;

to Randy Barney, Michael Baugher, Susan Brannan Walker, Heather Bryant, Elena Karina Byrne, Marcia Le Beau, Christina Cook, Lucia Galloway (and the Poetry at Claremont Library Reading Series), Carol Guess, Anna Leahy, Jeffrey Ethan Lee, Louise Mathias, Simone Muench, Farrah Field and Jared White (and Berl's Brooklyn Book Shop), and Andrew Wessels;

to the Squaw Valley Community of Writers and the Jeffery House gang: Heather Atfield, John Murillo, Sarah Pape, Leslie Seldin, Valerie Wallace, Javier Zamora (and Snoop Dogg's "agitate the gravel"… "get in where you fit in"… "I'm too swift on my toes/ to get caught up with you h***.").

Thanks to my family: Robbie Mehoke, Mary Tokita, and the memory of my parents, Robert and Barbara Mehoke.

Special thanks to Cati Porter and the Inlandia Institute for sharing the vision in creating the Hillary Gravendyk Prize as a memorial poetry book award and making dreams happen.

Much thanks for the support of What Books Press (and writers and supporters among their admirable collective, an inspirational force and treasure of the literary milieu), including: Sarah Maclay, Holaday Mason, Lynne Thompson, Gail Wronksy, Molly Bendall, Karen Kevorkian, Ash Good, and Gronk (an artist for all time!).

Thanks to Dorland Mountain Colony Art Colony where many of these poems were written.

AUTHOR'S NOTES

In the poem "Dear Hillary" the line "My favorite hobbies are archery and stamp collecting" is taken from the *Personality Assessment Inventory* developed by Leslie Morey (1991, 2007), a self-reporting personality test.

"Another Way To Say Your Name" was written in a collaborative series with Hillary Gravendyk. A companion poem, "Maureen," appears in *Mirror Inside Coffin* (Cherry Grove Collections, Wordtech Communications); Hillary's poem "Hillary, Hillary" appears in *Soluble Hour*, (Omnidawn), edited by Cynthia Arrieu-King. This poem spun from the original collaborations from the statement "Sometimes, When Alone, I Hear My Name" (an item from Cecil R. Reynolds, Randy W. Kamphaus, *Behavior Assessment System for Children, 3d ed.* (BASC-3). Additional collaborative poems in Gravendyk's *Soluble Hour* include: "Amazonite," "Sardonyx," "Sometimes When Alone, I Hear My Name." Alsop's collaborative poems—"Maureen," "Amazonite," and "Sardonyx"—appeared in *Mirror Inside Coffin*.

The poem "O improbable green. . ." was written in response to the Grottorossa Mummy (ca. 2d century AD): the sarcophagus of the mummy of a girl about eight years old. She is the second mummy to have been found in Rome, and is displayed on the first level below ground at the Museo Nazionale Romano-Palazzo Massimo alle Terme.

"Sky an Oar" sequence of poems includes references to dates the poems were written (i.e. VII/XII/MMXVI etc).

Sehnsucht is a German word translated (roughly) as "longing."

Táim sínte ar do thuama, translated from Gaelic, means "I am stretched on your grave." This title is taken from, and in response to, an anonymous traditional 17th-century ballad.

"Where Glass Shore's Light Wavers" is a ghost story (for serious!).

NOTES ON COLLABORATION

Collaboration process notes on Hillary are summarized in the poem "Glossopetrae," written in collaboration with Matteo Lexa (a second-grade student attending George Washington Charter Elementary School in Palm Desert, California, at the time). Collaborative poems (where noted in Acknowledgements), and several additional poems included here, honor the memory of Hillary Gravendyk (March 1, 1979-May 10, 2014), with gratitude for our friendship in love and admiration.

The poem "Sepiolite" was written as a memorial for Jody Lexa (October 22, 1956 - February 3, 2015).

With Brenda Hammack:
When I tripped across the bones in the dry creek bed I imagined the border, a space without sinew or stench—as when the elements polished the doe's skull, sternum, vertebrae to disclose beauty's articulate—as if a body's infinity lay in suspension among autumn's yellow enclosures: chinaberry, poisoned ash, cape lilac. Perhaps this was a postwar confession, as when you wrote: *never am I again.* The only channel between civilizations, violet wired fences, failed the town and the twelve fragrant dreams of the other. How did you answer the question. Where a girl and a sword forget the rattle-box measure of sky, twilight heron's iodine-colored feathers lingered at the gate. A pack-sled over sleep's rocks. I sent you a round. How did you answer the question. Night, neither a shadow's guess, his dust, nor the pond's red curdled seaweed. O wicked Sailor, the mixing water is ice-broken. Nevertheless, you'd said he was not familiar. Was he the same being? When I constructed the second message there was no more ledger. He was very sick by then. He never wanted to die. Savior to unequal reason. I recall death's best face. A surrealist's parlor game. The angle by which dead visualize you.

With Lissa Kiernan:
We stood at the bar, etched with initials almost discernible—drank through each wave's precipice. Pain's mysticism held an errant earring. We read the

current between mantlepiece portraits, the falling other in the other's son. Were our eyes able to ascertain what horizon arrived in the fold where each night the brigade planted a line of elms orphaned side by side? "What question was I…" She and I never told. The gates closed. And heat threaded each ventricle.

INDEX OF TITLES

Aggregate Turning Every Aspen	64
and when the hour leaves . . .	85
Another Way to Say Your Name	41
Apprentice	83
Archival Sparrows	28
Ballast	23
Blackout	22
Breathing into the next nearness . . .	70
Crimes Tonight	49
Dear Hillary,	20
[Elegy In Green Abatement: You Designate Seeing as the Seer]	71
Equuleus	38
Gabion	63
Chalmette {Through June In Dry Places, Generic Names}	72
Ghost Articulate	32
Glossopetrae	44
Guardian, Blue, Inez	30
I was the trauma inside betrayal . . .	48
January Itinerary, Parenthesis	35
Later Star, Late Blackness	66
Matins for Juliet	56
{Midnight Botanica: The Temple Is Reachable Only by a Bridge}	55
North Channel	36
Not portraits, not holy fire, . . .	81
O improbable green…	17
Oculus	80
Parenthesis Skyline	33
Pontiac	79
Promised	25
Prothalamion	54

Sacrament of Venus	24
Sacrestia	65
Scurvy, Birds	37
Sehnsucht	21
Selenomancy at Quadrature	53
Selenomancy In Summer Heat	77
Selenomancy Looking Southward	61
Selenomancy Where the Apparent Change in Size Is Due to the Eccentricity of Orbit	69
Selenomancy: Where the Apparent Wobbling of The Moon Is Known as Libration	19
Selenomancy Without Surface Pattern	47
Sepiolite	29
Sky an Oar, VII / XII / MMXIV	39
Sky an Oar, VIII/XI/MMXVI	57
Sky an Oar, X/XI/MMXIV	58
Sky an Oar, XIII/XII/MMXIV	74
Sky an Oar, XXV/IV/MMXIV	62
Sky an Oar, XXXI/VII/MMXVI	84
Snow Paradigm	26
Softly	78
Táim Sínte Ar Do Thuama	82
The antique hills half far . . .	15
The half-folded page . . .	45
The other way to write an elegy . . .	27
This was our knowledge . . .	50
Where Glass Shore's Light Wavers	40
[Why Loss Burns Back the Only Accompaniment Our Name Hardly Saves]	43
Witness	31

MAUREEN ALSOP, Ph.D., is the author of *Mirror Inside Coffin*; *Later, Knives & Trees*; *Mantic*; *Apparition Wren* (also a Spanish edition, *Reyezuelo Aparición*, translated by Mario Domínguez Parra); and several chapbooks (including: *Luminal Equation, the dream and the dream you spoke, 12 Greatest Hits, Nightingale Habit, Origin of Stone*). She is the winner of the Tony Quagliano International Poetry Award through the Hawaii Council for the Humanities, *Harpur Palate's* Milton Kessler Memorial Prize for Poetry, and *The Bitter Oleander's* Frances Locke Memorial Poetry Award. Her poems have been nominated for Pushcart Prizes on several occasions. Her poems, book reviews, essays, and visual poetics have appeared in *Memorious, The Laurel Review, AGNI, Blackbird, DIAGRAM, The Kenyon Review, Verse Daily, Rain Taxi, Mantis, Anomaly, Your Impossible Voice, Tupelo Quarterly, The Continental Review, The Journal of Compressed Arts*, The Riverside Art Museum, and Umbrella Studio among other journals, anthologies and venues. Her translations of *La pasajera/The Passenger* by Juana de Ibarbourou (Uruguay, 1892-1979) and poetry of Mario Domínguez Parra have appeared in *Box Car Review* and *Poetry Salzburg Review*. She teaches online with the Poetry Barn. She is a book review editor and associate poetry editor at *Poemeleon*. She holds an MFA from Vermont College.

LOS ANGELES

OTHER TITLES FROM WHAT BOOKS PRESS

ART

Gronk, A Giant Claw
Bilingual, spanish

Chuck Rosenthal, Gail Wronsky & Gronk,
Tomorrow You'll Be One of Us: Sci Fi Poems

PROSE

François Camoin, *April, May, and So On*

A.W. DeAnnuntis, *The Mysterious Islands and Other Stories*

Katharine Haake, *The Time of Quarantine*

Mona Houghton, *Frottage & Even As We Speak: Two Novellas*

Rod Val Moore, *Brittle Star*

Chuck Rosenthal, *Coyote O'Donohughe's History of Texas*

NON-FICTION

Chuck Rosenthal, *West of Eden: A Life in 21st Century Los Angeles*

POETRY

Kevin Cantwell, *One of Those Russian Novels*

Ramón García, *Other Countries*

Karen Kevorkian, *Lizard Dream*

Gail Wronsky, *Imperfect Pastorals*

WHATBOOKSPRESS.COM

www.ingramcontent.com/pod-product-compliance
Lightning Source LLC
Chambersburg PA
CBHW032046290426
44110CB00012B/978